C000083589

ASK0025195

ACKNOWLEDGEMENTS

A huge thank you to Yuri Prasad, Brian Richardson and Weyman Bennett. Without their help and hard work I would never have been able to write this.

Thanks to Esme Choonara, Eileen Short, Lina Nicolli and Peter Robinson who turned a huge piece of text into an actual book with some great pictures to go with it. Special thanks to Saba Shiraz who supported and encouraged me throughout.

ABOUT THE AUTHOR

Antony Hamilton is an anti-racist activist and member of the Socialist Workers' Party.

COVER IMAGE: Malcolm X speaking at an outdoor rally, probably in New York City, in 1963.

INSIDE FRONT: Malcolm sharing a joke with Muhammad Ali in February 1964 after Ali had become world heavyweight champion.

INSIDE BACK: Malcolm on a visit to Smethwick in Britain's West Midlands on 12 February 1965, nine days before he was killed.

Published by Bookmarks Publications 2016
ISBN print edition: 978-1-910885-12-3
ISBN Kindle: 978-1-910885-13-0
ISBN ePub: 978-1-910885-14-7
ISBN PDF: 978-1-910885-15-4
Typeset by Peter Robinson
Printed by Short Run Press Limited

A Rebel's Guide to
MALCOLM X

ANTONY HAMILTON

★1.
INTRODUCTION

In 2008 Barack Obama's election as the first ever Black president of the US sent shockwaves through American society. With the slogan "Yes We Can", he became for many millions of people a beacon of hope and progress.

For those who remembered the civil rights movement of the 1950s and 1960s and the focus on changing society by electing Black people into positions of power, this was the ultimate goal and a huge step forward in the campaign to end racism.

However, during two terms in office the Obama Administration failed to address the violent racism at the heart of the US judicial system and allowed space for far right groups and reactionary politics to grow.

The Black Lives Matter campaign, launched in 2013 to challenge the second class status of Black people in the US, gathered momentum following the killings of Eric Garner and Michael Brown in July and August 2014.

The campaign exposed police brutality and racism, and the electricity and energy of the demonstrations pulled in huge numbers of new activists. Protesters against racist policing felt that their demands for justice would at last be heard. But instead of backing the protesters, Obama chose to tell them that they had to accept the decision of the US justice system because the US was a "nation built on the rule of law" (www.whitehouse.gov/blog/2014/11/24/president-obama-delivers-statement-ferguson-grand-jurys-decision). For millions in the US this means the police can continue to murder Black people with impunity.

The mass marches, sit-ins and rallies against racism across the US have continued, inspiring solidarity from every corner of the world. This shockwave of resistance has resonated in the UK where there had already been major upheavals.

In 2011 the killing of Mark Duggan by the police sparked riots across England, unleashing tensions that had been building for years under immense levels of police harassment, brutality and racism. The Black Lives Matter campaign reinvigorated this resistance in a more coordinated way, with solidarity actions in cities across the UK which fundamentally challenged structural racism.

Within any anti-racist movement there are huge tactical questions to be faced about how we can bring about the change we need, including whether white people can be involved, whether Black people must lead and whether this system can be made to work for us or whether we need a different one.

Our rich history of struggle provides a crucial guide to answering these questions. We have many iconic figures who we can look to: Martin Luther King Jr, Maya Angelou, Frederick Douglass, Angela Davis, the Black Panthers and the American Communist Party (CP) of the 1920s and 1930s. But one of the most significant figures remains Malcolm X.

Malcolm was a Black revolutionary Muslim whose slogan of uncompromising militancy—"by any means necessary"—is still recognised all over the world. His life story shows how ideas can change with struggle. He was imprisoned, saved by religion and fought for Black separation. Later, as he travelled across Africa at a time of anti-colonial uprisings, he embraced integration and developed revolutionary ideas. His huge influence continued after his assassination; the Black Power movement was built on the back of his achievements. He exposed the link between capitalism and racism with a charismatic flair that left his opponents stunned.

Half a century after Malcolm's assassination, we are still fighting a battle against an unjust system. At the end of the first Black presidency, the election campaign has seen Republican candidate Donald Trump call Mexicans rapists and demand a ban on Muslims entering the US. In Europe refugees, immigrants and Muslims are the targets of racism, labelled as terrorists and blamed for the failings of capitalism.

The need to take forward Malcolm's arguments and militancy is as strong as ever. And, as Malcolm's own political journey shows, ultimately we need to challenge the system itself.

★ 2. EARLY LIFE AND GARVEYISM

Malcolm X is remembered by many for his revolutionary zeal, uncompromising attitude and militant spirit. He is one of the most iconic figures of Black Power and represented a radical edge of Black politics, which drew inspiration from anti-colonial struggles and cut through to the civil rights movement. However, he wasn't born with an understanding of the world and knowing he would fight with everything he had to change it. He wasn't even born as Malcolm X.

He was born Malcolm Little into a very poor family on 19 May 1925 in Omaha, Nebraska.

Although they lived in the Midwest—in a state with no specific segregation laws—Malcolm's family still suffered regular attacks by the white supremacist Ku Klux Klan (KKK) and harassment by the police. Holding down a job and keeping a roof over their heads was a constant struggle.

Malcolm was the fourth of seven children born to the Reverend Earl Little Sr and Louise Little. He also had three half siblings from Earl's first marriage. This large family strained his parents' ability to provide for their children and stay strong in the face of adversity. Louise later paid the toll of this emotional burden.

Earl and Louise were both political activists in Marcus Garvey's United Negro Improvement Association (UNIA).

The UNIA was a Black nationalist group whose programme set out to organise capitalism in the interests of Black people. They set up Black only businesses, banks and housing associations and pulled a community together around a network of churches. The aim of the programme was to carve out a space for Black people in a racist society. In this sense it challenged racism, albeit in a very limited way, in the face of constant attacks from the state and white supremacists.

Garvey believed that the task for Black people was to return to Africa and build a better world for themselves there. This was based on a belief that all Black people had the same interests and left to themselves would create a Black utopia. It is from this tradition that Malcolm would later draw political inspiration.

The UNIA had a huge attraction in the northern ghettos where, even though segregation was officially abolished, Black people were forced to live separately. Businesses were set up by Black people to serve Black people. This atmosphere of self-reliance played into the ideology of Garvey who believed Black people needed to better themselves and their own communities in order to progress.

In the South the ideas of the UNIA grew organically out of the extreme levels of oppression. Black people had already been ostracised as second class citizens within their own states and the UNIA provided moments of brief escape and a long-term goal to fight for. Weekly UNIA meetings instilled the confidence and militancy needed to deal with daily persecution by the state and the KKK. Meetings were delivered in churches by a local reverend and were a hub of pride and inspiration. The collective strength drawn from powerful sermons reached their climax when everyone would join together to sing "Up You Mighty Race". The lyrics spoke to the reality of racial oppression, recognised all Black people as one common people and gave the courage to fight all together for what is right:

"How long must our people be a human sacrifice/ Stand up, defend your rights/ Up, up ye mighty race, you can accomplish what you will/ Stand up, defend your rights".

By the 1920s Garvey could claim the UNIA had 6 million members. Although this is probably an overestimate, his newspaper had a circulation of up to 200,000 and claimed 35,000 fee-paying members in New York City alone. At its peak there were at least 700 branches of the UNIA across 38 states.

During the 1920s and 1930s Garvey's Black nationalist movement was not the only challenge to racism; the left too was organising.

Under the slogan "an injury to one is an injury to all", the Industrial Workers of the World (IWW) organised strikes, mass meetings, and parades and focused on direct action and sabotage. The IWW grew with the workers' struggle throughout the 1910s, pushing on following the Russian Revolution in 1917. State attacks, defeats in the early 1920s and the IWW's rejection of political parties led to a long-term decline in membership and activity. However, their struggle inspired and paved the way for organisations like the Communist Party (CP) and others.

The Russian Revolution was transformative and provided a huge source of inspiration for many and a major attraction for early recruits of the CP. The newly founded CP prioritised recruiting Black workers. Radicals from all over the world were encouraged to travel to Russia and see the new society at first hand. Among the hundreds of Americans who made the trip in the early 1920s were a handful of Black activists. Lovett Fort-Whiteman believed it was, "the first state in the history of the world which had actually solved the problem of racial discrimination". Homer Smith recalled: "If a Negro was standing in line at a shop, some Russian was sure to tug him by the arm and lead him to the front of the line. If it was a matter of a dance with a Russian girl, a Russian man would always give way" (Joy Gleason Carew, *Blacks, Reds, and the Russians: Sojourners in Search of the Soviet Promise*, Rutgers University Press, 2010).

The CP's first major test was in 1929 in Gastonia, North Carolina, when the National Textile Workers Union called a strike. The CP organised integrated meetings with Black strikers speaking—at a time when mainstream unions barely allowed Black workers to join. Party organisers, Black and white, were sent from New York to help the struggle. Bosses understood the threat. Not only were strikers demanding better wages, they also wanted to break the segregation that served the rich so well.

Company police broke picket lines and meetings with clubs and organisers were shot at. Although the strike was eventually defeated, the knowledge that Black and white workers could strike together, even in the South, spread like wildfire. It showed that white workers could be broken from racism, providing no concessions were made to it.

Not long after, in Alabama in 1931, the CP led the

campaign to free the Scottsboro boys, nine Black teenagers falsely convicted of rape and sentenced to death. The prosecutor famously told the jury, "Guilty or not, let's get rid of these niggers". This case was widely recognised as legal lynching and groups of white men organised in order to "defend" white women. Black people were facing the violence of the state and the violence of thugs on the street.

Throughout the 1930s the method used by the CP showed how to fight racism effectively: mass marches and rallies by Black and white people with Black and white speakers on platforms. This unity sent a shiver through the establishment as well as providing a counterweight to Garvey and separation.

This was the background to Malcolm's early childhood as the Little family moved around the Midwest to set up local branches, building up organisation and recruiting to the of the UNIA. However, for an activist family danger was never far away; the KKK was systematic in its attacks on Black political activists and leaders.

The family was forced to move many times. Malcolm remembered his house being firebombed when he was only four years old: "suddenly snatched awake into a frightening confusion of pistol shots and shouting and smoke and flames" (*The Autobiography of Malcolm X* with the assistance of Alex Haley, p81, Penguin Books, 2001).

It was in Lansing, Michigan, that the goal of the local KKK was realised. Malcolm was only six when his father's body was found left in the middle of the road. For those who knew him, there was never any doubt that he was killed in a racist attack.

It wasn't long before the burden of childcare, work

and racism overwhelmed Louise and some of the children were taken into care. Malcolm was moved between different families but was able to visit his mother and siblings fairly frequently. By 1939 Louise had suffered a breakdown and was admitted to a mental hospital, where she remained until 1963. Malcolm and his siblings now only had each other for support.

At school Malcolm was a good pupil. He repeatedly came top of his class. But the racism of the US in the 1930s oozed like a disease into every section of society and was reinforced through institutions. One day Malcolm was asked by his history teacher what career he would like. When Malcolm responded, "I've been thinking I'd like to be a lawyer", his teacher was surprised and said: "you've got to be realistic... that's no realistic goal for a nigger" (Manning Marable, *Malcolm X a Life of Reinvention*, p38, Penguin Books, 2011).

This confirmed for Malcolm something he had long felt; he wasn't the same as his white classmates, he wasn't held in the same regard and he was destined to never be as great—regardless of his academic achievements.

★ 3: THE GREAT MIGRATION AND LIFE IN THE GHETTOS

For Black people, life in the Northern cities offered the possibility of prosperity and advancement, something that the legacy of slavery in the South hadn't allowed. The political terrain also had stark differences. In the North Black people participated much more openly in political activity. Although Black workers were not allowed to join most trade unions, they agitated in Black nationalist organisations and alongside their white counterparts in the CP. Although they were routinely attacked by the police, it was a much easier fight than in the South where white supremacists would regularly lynch and murder Black activists.

The so-called Jim Crow laws passed in the South in the late 1870s set up a system of legal segregation that rigidly divided every aspect of life. Whites were encouraged to think of themselves as superior, despite the fact that most lived in poverty while the rich enjoyed big profits and unchallenged power.

The Jim Crow laws carved Black people out of jobs, homes and education. In the North segregation wasn't legal, however, Black people were pushed into the worst housing which became ghettos ignored by the state. They had the worst living conditions, which encouraged disease and extreme poverty and the jobs available were severely limited to the tedious, menial or dangerous.

For millions of Black Americans however, the North shone as a beacon of hope and an escape from the lynching, murder and daily persecution as second class citizens.

This is why the early and mid-20th century in the US was characterised by periods of mass migration, where Black people in the southern states moved in huge numbers to northern cities.

The first large movement was during the First World War when 454,000 Black southerners moved north. The demand for workers was the result of 5 million men leaving to serve in the armed forces and restrictions on immigration. Some industries were so desperate for workers that they would pay Black people to migrate north.

In the 1920s, another 800,000 Black people left the South, followed by 398,000 in the 1930s. Between 1940 and 1960 more than 3,348,000 Black people left the South for northern and western cities.

In 1941 Malcolm made his journey to the city of Boston and in 1942 to Harlem (New York City). It was in these cities that Malcolm's small town experience hit a major contrast.

Here he saw huge numbers of Black people living together, running their own businesses and playing in bands without the threat of the KKK. The music, community and freedom of the city pulled him in.

He was also shocked by the levels of integration. The small Midwestern town Malcolm grew up in was an alien world compared to the major industrial cities where—although still frowned upon—there were interracial relationships.

The experience changed him and he could no longer accept the taunts of his white classmates or the racism of his teachers. In his biography he says he "drew away from white people" (*The Autobiography*, p119).

Malcolm was only 15 when he left Lansing, Michigan, to move in with Ella. Although she enrolled him in a local school, he only attended once before dropping out and started to look for work. He did odd jobs such as shining shoes and selling sandwiches on the trains. It wasn't long before Malcolm grew tired of menial low-paid jobs and he was pulled into the "flashy world of bars and clubs" that Boston offered (Marable, p43). Although there were many more work possibilities in the North for Black people, only a small percentage of Black people were able to accumulate enough wealth to pull themselves out of poverty or start their own businesses. For the majority of people these dreams were perpetually out of reach.

Malcolm—like many other Black people who couldn't escape the ghettos—learned about the world of drugs, gambling and pimping. He developed a flare for racketeering.

With this change of environment, his looks changed as well. When he had turned up on Ella's doorstep his hair was "cut hick style". But only months after his entrance into Black metropolitan society—on the advice of his new best friend, hustler and companion in Boston street life

"Shorty" Jarvis—he started styling his hair into a "conk"; it "was the emblem of the hippest, street-savvy Black, the choice of hustlers, pimps, professional gamblers, and criminals" (Marable, p43). He was wearing zoot suits, "an act of defiance against white standards of behaviour" and doing the lindy hop, "the standard dance performed to syncopated big band jazz" (Marable, p45).

Malcolm embraced the cultural difference of the Black ghettos, but this was also a route to economic freedom. In the ghetto he could run numbers rackets, deal drugs and pick up odd jobs to supplement his erratic income. This would have been impossible where he grew up, not only for fear of being lynched, but also because jobs were scarce and there were extremely limited possibilities for promotion or advancement. The luxury of this freedom fed into Malcolm's vision of how to get by in American society; it was all about being fast and evading responsibility. Only later in his life would he develop an understanding of exploitation and how to tackle it head on.

Alongside Shorty, another Black man known as "Sonny" and three white women—Bea Caragulian (whom Malcolm had an on and off sexual relationship with); her younger sister, Joyce; and Armenian born Kora Marderosian—Malcolm made plans to rob homes in the wealthier neighbourhoods. Over a month the gang was able to steal from eight houses before Malcolm slipped up and was caught selling a stolen watch and in possession of a loaded gun. He revealed the names of all the gang members under interrogation, however, Sonny was able to escape.

The intense racism at the heart of US courtrooms was

obvious from the start of Malcolm's trial. Malcolm and Shorty were both referred to as "*schvartze* [German for Black] bastards" by one lawyer and Shorty was told he "had no business associating with white women". The women were called "poor, unfortunate...scared lost girls". Malcolm also claimed that the district attorney had unsuccessfully tried "to get the girls to testify that we raped them" (Marable, p68).

In 1946, Shorty and Malcolm, who was 19 at the time, were sentenced to between eight and ten years' imprisonment, while Bea was sentenced to five years, of which she served seven months. The injustice delivered on that day left a scar on Malcolm and also shook his trust in women and accomplices.

★ 4: PRISON AND THE NATION OF ISLAM

During this period Malcolm underwent a remarkable change, from the street savvy wannabe gangster to a devout religious follower. Prison laid the foundations for his political education and development, but it was the Nation of Islam (NOI) that completely transformed the way he saw the world.

In prison Malcolm made friends with another inmate, John Elton Bembry, whose superior intellect and impressive string of thefts won Malcolm's respect. After some hesitation, Malcolm began a process of self-development, enrolling on various university courses; he saw education as a way out of the terrible conditions of Charlestown Prison. He also began to develop his speaking style by reading about linguistics. In January 1947 he was transferred to the Massachusetts Reformatory at Concord, which was marginally better than Charlestown. Here the visits from family and friends picked up again and Ella convinced herself that Malcolm was undergoing a positive transformation.

In early 1948 Malcolm received a letter from his

brother Philbert; this was the first attempt to recruit Malcolm to the NOI. He initially dismissed the letter, but when a second letter came—this time from another brother, Reginald—it caught his interest. The letter contained a few instructions with an appealing promise at the end: "Malcolm, don't eat any more pork, and don't smoke any more cigarettes. I'll show you how to get out of prison" (*The Autobiography*, p249).

The NOI was a Black separatist organisation led by Elijah Muhammed. It was not connected to mainstream Islam and preached that white people were the product of a genetic experiment by an evil Black scientist called Yacub and that their time on Earth was coming to an end. Set up in 1930 amid the great depression, the founder Wallace D Fard believed the task for Black people was to separate themselves from white society and prepare for Judgement Day. The NOI held huge appeal for people who were persecuted and marginalised. It built support through networks of Black businesses and mosques which bolstered racial pride and gave refuge and support to the victims of a racist system.

As an anti-white force that focused on self-improvement, the NOI's ideology fundamentally challenged the second class status of Black people and provided rigid structures of improvement that helped many gain their freedom. They believed in the oneness of God, Allah, who was Black. This was a vastly influential tool which the NOI could use to attract disillusioned Black people who felt like they didn't belong. A Black God—at a time when it was unheard of to see a Black person in a governmental position, let alone a divine one—was a radical rejection of Christianity and American society.

It is little wonder that these ideas proved attractive to so many.

The people they attracted were usually the poorest and most disenfranchised sections of the Black working class; their separatism put off sections of the Black petit-bourgeoisie who were committed to working their way up the system.

As for those who were lost to prison, drugs and crime, the NOI offered an alternative world which recognised them and gave them opportunities they had never had.

They held events inside their religious temples that focused on internal education. The men took up the positions of influence and power in the sect while women occupied a secondary place. This fitted with Malcolm's views: he saw his mother as weak because of her mental health problems and the white prostitutes in Boston and Harlem as an example of the nature of women.

Each temple had a minister, an officer to lead the local branch of the Fruit of Islam (FOI)—the paramilitary wing of the NOI—and a woman to lead the Muslim Girls Training.

By 1948 Ella had managed to have Malcolm transferred to Norfolk Prison Colony, which he described as "a heaven". Malcolm met with Reginald not long after his transfer. He told Malcolm of the Black God and the nature of the "white devil". What he heard made Malcolm question every white person he'd ever known, which reaffirmed that what Reginald was saying must be true. He thought of those who "killed my father...calling my mother crazy...the cops... the judge who gave me ten years" and all those who had denied him opportunity, discarded his trust and shut him away. The oppressor became ever more the face of "the devil white man" (*The Autobiography*, p254).

This path of rejecting white society became more convincing to Malcolm the more visits he received from Reginald and other family members who had also joined local temples. In order to comprehend the new information Malcolm threw himself into education and drew inspiration from the stories which his family was teaching him. He read the history of the trans-Atlantic slave trade, W E B Du Bois and African-American revolts and found his passion for speaking in the prison debating club. No matter what the topic was, Malcolm would throw himself into it. It was here that he developed his famous, distinctive oratorical style which later proved so captivating.

In 1949 Reginald was expelled from the NOI. Malcolm wrote a letter to Elijah Muhammed in protest against the decision. The furious reply he received along with what Malcolm later believed to be a vision of "Master W D Fard, the Messiah" by his bedside, secured his belief in the NOI and reinforced his devotion. After this he began to agitate inside prison for access to books from Black authors and rights for Muslim prisoners. He also changed his name to Malcolm X; members of the NOI used the surname X to reject the name given to them during the slave trade. After a period of devoted service, members would be given a Muslim name by Elijah Muhammed linking them to the Shabazz tribe.

This was a monumental transformation and would mark the first major shift in Malcolm's political consciousness. Whereas previously he had been the victim of the system, always manoeuvring to avoid responsibility, now he was actively challenging it and trying to figure out where the root of the problem for Black people in America was. He convinced himself he needed a "revolution in his identities and beliefs" (Marable, p79).

During this period Malcolm repeatedly wrote to Charlestown officials in order to be paroled for early release. In August 1952 (six years into his sentence) he was finally released and took up a full time job alongside his brother Wilfred.

Now out of prison, Malcolm didn't waste any time. He attended his first meeting at the Detroit chapter of the NOI (known as Temple No 1) and was angry at the small size of the congregation. From there he travelled in a ten-car convoy to see Elijah Muhammed speak in person and, in front of several hundred members, Elijah called out Malcolm personally for his devotion while inside prison.

After a series of jobs and the end to his probation, Malcolm began working for the NOI. His vibrancy and charisma made him the perfect voice of the NOI. His past as a hustler and the language he used made him easy to relate to. He was in touch with the conditions of the poorest Black people and able to articulate anger into an organisational weapon.

At the end of 1953 Elijah Muhammed selected Malcolm to serve as a minister in Boston. Malcolm was successful in his recruitment campaign and was able to set up the Temple No 11. Following this impressive performance, and in the footsteps of his Garveyite father, Malcolm was sent around to different states in order to build support in Black communities. His influence was tremendous and he rallied the NOI from an obscure sect with a membership of hundreds into an organisation tens of thousands strong. In 1954 he became the minister for Harlem's

Temple No 7 and began to be recognised as a national figure. Harlem was Malcolm's home; he understood the people and how to engage mass rallies. His dynamism grew from the energy and excitement of his addresses in which he slandered white authority and built a reputation as a fierce debater.

He rose to prominence by reaching out to the most disaffected Black people and his public addresses on street corners could gather thousands. He marched members of the FOI to a police station and ordered the release of two of his own members who had been arrested after defending themselves from racist police officers.

From that moment until his assassination the FBI would follow him wherever he went.

While Malcolm's reputation was building as a devoted follower who could get the job done, it was also causing serious tensions with the leadership of the NOI. As Malcolm progressed, Elijah began to treat him with greater privileges than any other member and in the eyes of the media Malcolm was considered equal to the leadership of the NOI. In particular Raymond Sharrieff, Louis Farrakhan and John Ali, who reflected the most conservative elements of the NOI, grew to feel threatened by the power which Malcolm represented. However, the tension between them was political, not personal.

Malcolm intervened more and more on the political topics of the day, speaking as a representative and pushing the NOI towards the people drawn into the civil rights movement. The NOI rejected involvement in any political act because they saw it as a justification of the system they lived in; their aim was complete separation not involvement. Malcolm's agitation was winning him layers of new Black Muslims, but he was heading down a road which would lead him into direct opposition with people of significantly higher influence in the sect.

Most famously in 1959 in a TV documentary called *The Hate that Hate Produced*, Malcolm said: "When someone sticks a knife into my back nine inches and then pulls it out six inches they haven't done me any favour. They should not have stabbed me in the first place... During slavery they inflicted the most extreme form of brutality against us to break our spirit, to break our will...after they did all this to us for 310 years, then they come up with some so-called Emancipation Proclamation... And today the white man actually runs around here thinking he is doing Black people a favour."

With this and many other appearances, Malcolm caused ripples in the conservative NOI leadership who would later rally against him.

★ 5:
THE
CIVIL
RIGHTS
MOVEMENT
AND
MALCOLM

The 1950s and 1960s were explosive. The civil rights movement, as Bob Dylan sang, proved that "the times they are a changin"!

The system that had dominated the South since the end of the Civil War was under a sustained attack. Black people who once cowered were emboldened and fighting back. People were sitting in, riding, defying and the old order was terrified. They were determined to resist. The result was mass confrontation and a violent racist reaction.

In December 1955 Rosa Parks, a young Black woman in Montgomery, Alabama, was arrested for refusing to give up her seat to a white man on a public bus. Her action sparked a year-long bus boycott that launched the campaign against segregation into a national movement capable of mobilising millions of people. It was during the Montgomery bus boycott that Martin Luther King Jr came to prominence as a civil rights leader. His standing as a local reverend gave him a level of respect and influence among the different layers of the Black community that would shape the politics of the movement.

Southern Black churches, led by ministers such as King, played a central role in the civil rights movement. Ministers spoke from the pulpit and street corners quoting biblical passages about suffering that resonated with people living under segregation. A brave and determined movement grew up which, drawing on Gandhi's strategy of non-violence, stood up for itself but didn't strike back. These non-violent tactics served as a means of widening the movement by offering a more "legitimate" route to change.

The rejection of violence popularised the fight for civil rights across most of the South as Black people facing the KKK, racist police and lynch mobs were offered an avenue to protest against injustice. Civil rights leaders thought non-violence would reduce the threat of violent retaliation. However, it became painfully obvious the state's response would be anything but non-violent.

The footage of peaceful Black protesters facing cruel violence at the hands of the Southern cops would come to define the bravery of civil rights activists. The movement was characterised by small victories aimed at the long-term goal of changing the law. It focused on shaming the US in the eyes of the world, on showing that the government could hardly call themselves leaders of the world's most free and equal society when they denied basic rights to their own people.

Malcolm was critical of the non-violent tactics, supporting the right of self-defence. He said: "Be peaceful, be courteous, obey the law, respect everyone; but if someone puts a hand on you, send him to the cemetery" ("Message to the Grassroots", November 1963) and "if we react to white racism with a violent reaction, to me that's no Black racism. If you come to put a rope around my neck and I hang you for it, to me that's not racism. Yours is racism, but my reaction has nothing to do with racism" (Ahmed Shawki, *Black Liberation and Socialism*, Haymarket, 2006, p173)

Central to the movement was the National Association for the Advancement of Colored People (NAACP) set up in 1909 by white descendants of abolitionists and Black activists including W E B Du Bois as a grassroots civil rights organisation. It actively campaigns for unity among Black and white people in order to fight racism and states that it "seeks to remove all barriers of racial discrimination through the democratic processes". Rosa Parks, for example, was not simply a tired seamstress who spontaneously stood up for herself; she was an NAACP member who led the coordinated action. The NAACP also played a hugely supportive role in Little Rock to secure desegregated education for nine Black students as well as helping to organise the 1963 March on Washington.

The civil rights movement was able to bring together all elements of anti-racist activity and perfectly capture the anger that Black people felt about their unequal status. It gained momentum because the movement was everywhere, representing a multitude of things to different groups of people, from soldiers denied their basic rights after risking their lives in the two world wars and later Vietnam, to the countless riots across the northern ghettos against police brutality.

As the civil rights movement took aim at Washington young people took to the streets on a daily basis to take on segregation in their own towns and cities. Most famous were the Greensboro sit-ins in 1960 when a group of students sat in a Woolworth department store restaurant and refused to move. This direct action taken against segregation struck a blow at the heart of the southern states. By the end of March the movement had spread to 55 cities in 13 states and by July the sit-ins were forcing the department store to change its policy. It became a source of inspiration and excitement for ordinary Black people across the US.

Then came the freedom riders, who fought to desegregate interstate transport by forcing Washington to uphold federal law against racist state laws. The rides involved mainly northern activists travelling south through the segregated states. Along the way they were met with horrific violence from white mobs that burnt buses and attacked the protesters, while others were beaten up by police and thrown into cells. The brutality didn't stop them and the riders made it onto national TV and into newspapers, making them a magnet for young activists.

A generation of young people were being drawn into the struggle day by day and the Student Non-Violent Coordinating Committee (SNCC) was ready to lead the charge. Malcolm was initially quite disdainful of the radicals but understood their potential and the energy they injected into the movement. He wanted to make his presence known among these people and spread the message of the NOI.

The greatest achievement of the civil rights movement was its ability to cast its net so wide, inspiring new groups and younger people to engage in political struggle. But, as with all movements that challenge the state, it came up against major obstacles and strategy was the main source of division.

1963 was a big year for the movement; the planned march on Washington was a way of targeting the campaign directly at the White House. But what started off as a radical chance to shut down the capital with sit-ins was quickly taken over by the conservative elements of the leadership and welcomed by the Democratic Party. They demanded that the radical elements be controlled and the march turned into a celebration of the government. For months prior to the march there were arguments about the route, who should speak and in what order. The FBI were running a tight ship, undercover police were ready to make arrests, hundreds of spaces were made available in nearby jail cells and every speech had to be screened. It seemed like the militancy was draining from the movement.

But what couldn't be foreseen was the strength of the demonstration. On 28 August 1963, 250,000 people marched on Washington for jobs and freedom with slogans for effective civil rights and an end to racial segregation. John Lewis of the SNCC wanted to say John F Kennedy had done "too little, too late", but his speech was censored.

Nevertheless, he received huge applause after saying: "We will splinter the segregated South into a thousand pieces and put them back together in the image of God and democracy... We cannot stop, and we will not be patient."

The strength of the demonstration resonated around the world, but it would take more action before Kennedy's administration would do anything.

Only one month after the demonstration there was a church bombing in Birmingham, Alabama, which killed four young girls and injured many more. This was a racist reaction to the strength of the civil rights movement and Malcolm saw this as a vindication of his ideas, that white people did not want equality or integration. This sparked increased calls for Black self-defence and armed resistance.

Despite the rise in the popular struggle for equal rights, the NOI ordered its members to eschew the movement which was seen as a distraction from the end goal of a separate Black society.

Malcolm X described the demonstration as the "Farce on Washington". He said: "Yes, I was there... Who ever heard of angry revolutionists all harmonising 'We Shall Overcome'...with the very people they were supposed to be angrily revolting against?... How was a one-day 'integrated' picnic going to counter-influence these representatives of prejudice rooted deep in the psyche of the American white man for four hundred years?" (*The Autobiography*, p388.)

With this speech against the demonstration Malcolm was drawing out existing frustration with the slow speed of change which the civil rights movement was bringing. But he was able to spin it and blame all white people involved, saying that they were the enemy. He called the Black leaders of the movement "Uncle Toms", accusing them of abandoning the cause of Black people in return for positions of power and purposefully deceiving them by working with whites.

This summed up a feeling of resentment which some of the more radical elements of the movement felt after the March on Washington. The march was intended to turn a spotlight onto the white liberals in government who said they opposed segregation but did nothing. However it ended up being a celebration of those people.

Malcolm, whose politics had been developing before 1963, became the most eloquent spokesman of this rejection of integration.

The main crux of the argument following the March on Washington was that the civil rights movement was taking too long to bring about change. For example the Supreme Court ruled in 1955 that all schools should be integrated, but ten years later 75 percent of schools in the South were still segregated. The SNCC became increasingly radical and disillusioned with the legal battle which King and others were waging. John Lewis was a leading member and began agitating around riots in Birmingham and voter registration in Selma. These became bitter battles with the police, leading to hundreds of arrests.

The civil rights movement was entering a new phase. There was division between those who stuck by the Democrats and denounced the violence of the rioters and those who took up slogans of Black Power, blaming white liberalism for the movement's dead end; it wasn't long before some blamed all whites.

Malcolm's militancy and his insistence that all white people were "devils" set him apart from the movement in its early years, but as a new generation of radicals began to break with the non-violent leadership he found a growing audience for his ideas. Malcolm was able to position himself as a radical voice in the campaign against police violence, slum landlords and businesses of the North, as well as the institutional racism in the South. In countless meetings and interviews he articulated the anger and alienation of Black people. He used his position as minister of Temple No 7 to speak on platforms alongside other Black activists involved in civil rights. It wasn't unusual for Malcolm to stand on a street corner and draw a crowd of hundreds if not thousands.

The civil rights movement was defined by its multira- cial composition and opened a debate about the nature of racism and who could be part of opposing it. With many young white activists drawn into the movement, it raised serious questions about the strategy of the NOI.

The politics of separation were based on an under- standing of oppression defined by individual power relations which saw all white people as the perpetrators of racism—whether it be racist comments on the street, white judges and police officers criminalising Black peo- ple or abuse and violence from individuals or organised white supremacist groups.

This was understandable, in a context where liberals in government used the movement as a platform for their own politics and denounced anyone involved in violence, regardless of the institutional violence waged against Black people. President Kennedy himself, for example, tried to stop the freedom riders. He said to Harris Wofford, a Justice Department official: "Can't you get your goddamned friends off those buses?" (Raymond Arsenault, *Freedom Riders: 1961 and the Struggle for Racial Justice*, OUP, 2006, p114.)

Such attitudes strengthened Malcolm's position, which was based on a misunderstanding of who benefited from racism. White workers are tricked into believing they have more in common with their white bosses than their Black co-workers. In reality capitalism rests on the exploitation of workers of all colours and everyone is worse off where there are higher levels of racism.

★ 6: MALCOLM SPLITS WITH THE NATION OF ISLAM

Malcolm began to see the limits of the NOI at the height of his political career. As a national minister he regularly intervened on behalf of the NOI but was routinely pulled back into line by the leadership when speaking on political issues. He was torn between the radical pull of the civil rights movement and the conservatism of the NOI.

He later explained in his autobiography: "privately I was convinced that our Nation Of Islam could be an even greater force in the American Black man's overall struggle—if we engaged in more action" and "It could be heard increasingly in the Negro communities: 'Those Muslims talk tough, but they never do anything, unless somebody bothers Muslims.'" (*The Autobiography*, p397.)

Malcolm's attempts to balance his political involvement and his duty to his Temple stretched him to his limits, while hostility towards him grew among a section of the NOI leadership, encouraged mainly by John Ali and

Captain Joseph. They represented the most conservative elements of the NOI and would eventually lead the hostile faction in an attempt to remove any positive trace of Malcolm from the NOI.

The tensions within the NOI and in the movement outside it continued to build throughout the early 1960s in the shadow of the Vietnam War and popular protests against it.

Malcolm's split from the NOI seemed inevitable. Hostility inside the Nation added to his growing uncertainty about Elijah Muhammed's divinity and leadership. From 1961 rumours began to gain momentum about Elijah Muhammed's illegitimate children with the various secretaries he had personally hired from within the NOI.

Amid this turmoil President Kennedy was assassinated. When he was killed, Elijah Muhammed personally ordered all his ministers to mourn quietly and not say anything to the press. However Malcolm saw this as an opportunity to air his frustration at the US government and he refused to join the mourning of the NOI. A week after the assassination, in Temple No 7 to an audience of several hundred including the national press, he likened the death of the President to "the chickens coming home to roost" and "being an old farm boy myself, chickens coming home to roost never did make me sad, they've always made me glad". In other words, all the horrors and atrocities that the US had exported across the world had come back to bite them.

This statement shook the NOI, which feared a backlash from the state. This set in motion the case from the faction hostile to Malcolm to have him expelled.

He was suspended for the next 90 days. This sentence

was much harsher than usual and clearly an attempt by a section of the leadership to set in motion Malcolm's removal. It became quite apparent during this time that the leadership of the NOI was never going to allow Malcolm to return. If a member was suspended they had the right to a fair trial in front of the other members of their Temple, however Malcolm wasn't offered this.

In his absence Louis Farrakhan, Raymond Sharrieff and other leading members began circulating rumours inside the temples in order to make Malcolm so unwanted that he could never return. Although numerous stories were spread about Malcolm, they all came to a similar conclusion: "If you knew what the Minister did, you'd go out and kill him yourself."

Malcolm pulled his friends close during this time to build up a level of respectability in the NOI. Closest of all was boxer Cassius Clay, better known as Muhammad Ali, who had been inspired by hearing Malcolm speak and was being promoted as the next big fighter; an underdog who could take on Sonny Liston, widely regarded as unbeatable.

The NOI didn't care for Clay since they saw popular culture—such as playing in bands and professional fighting—as beneath them. When Clay challenged Liston, Malcolm supported Clay, planting ideas of his imminent victory based on his devotion to Islam.

In February 1964 Clay beat Liston and the world was stunned.

The publicity became a pole of attraction for the NOI leadership. In a press conference following the fight Clay rejected his last name and became known as Cassius X, admitting his loyalties to the NOI. Elijah Muhammad latched onto this, recognising the world's greatest fighter was now openly one of the Black Muslims. Elijah gave Cassius X the name Muhammad Ali. Just a week later Malcolm formally announced his split with the NOI and Cassius was ripped away from him.

This was possibly the most antagonistic name he could have given in light of the media hysteria over the fight. Now the world's greatest fighter was challenging the "white devils" with a name that packed a punch as big as his.

By 1964 the momentum and determination of the civil rights movement forced the US Congress to pass the Civil Rights Act and later a Voting Rights Act (1965). This formally outlawed racial discrimination and Jim Crow segregation, but failed to dent the everyday racism that blighted the lives of the majority of Black people. It also didn't change much in the North where segregation laws didn't exist but Black people were still kept separate.

At the same time Malcolm had reached a dead end, there was no way back into the organisation he had dedicated his life to building. In March 1964 Malcolm officially resigned from the NOI. He said: "I am prepared to cooperate in local civil rights actions in the South and elsewhere...to heighten the political consciousness of Negroes and intensify their identification against white society." (Marable, p293.) He had thrown away the religious rhetoric with an overtly political statement, reinforcing that his break with the Nation was political and not personal; however he still held on to a belief in Black separation.

Malcolm wasted no time in setting up alternative organisations following his break from the NOI. While he influenced sections of the movement under the slogans of Black pride and self-organisation, the movement also influenced him. This dialectical relationship would propel Malcolm through immense changes and developments during the last year of his life.

However, the split wasn't easy for Malcolm. He had been arguing for years with people who represented different sections of Black politics, but he'd always had the line from the NOI to back him up. Now he needed to formulate his own thoughts and present himself on the political stage once again.

Before setting out for his Hajj (a holy pilgrimage to Mecca which all Muslims should complete once in their lives) and immediately following the split he set up the Muslim Mosque Inc. (MMI). This mirrored the NOI and was Malcolm's attempt to maintain a level of organisation which would hold together his followers during his political and spiritual journey. Malcolm used his Hajj and trips to Africa to connect the MMI to the rest of the Islamic world.

He wanted to create separate Muslim and political organisations to maintain a breadth to organising which would have been impossible under the old NOI banner. Doing this he could rally his loyal supporters in the MMI and be recognised in the international Muslim community, while also campaigning with civil rights activists and revolutionaries in the US and Africa.

Malcolm sent letters from his Hajj knowing full well that they would be widely read and would cause a stir among his followers. In his letters he describes converting to orthodox Sunni Islam and breaking down the barriers between Black and white people. He rejected the ways of the NOI and opened his arms to alternative methods of organising alongside civil rights leaders and white progressives.

Malcolm had travelled the same path for Elijah Muhammed years before in order to further the name of the NOI and connect the Nation to the wider Islamic world. The people he met along the way encouraged his development but were wary of the NOI teachings, specifically Elijah's claim to be a prophet and that Fard, their founder, was Allah personified. This time Malcolm would be travelling free of any organisational ties, a development that would greatly help his political transformation.

★ 7: BECOMING A REVOLUTIONARY IN AN ERA OF PAN-AFRICANISM

When Malcolm set out to undergo his Hajj he drew up a map of northern Africa and the Middle East. He aimed to visit many of the states he had been welcomed into the first time around and some more.

The experience would challenge his long-held belief about "white devils". His first stop was Cairo. When he got off the plane there were "throngs of people, obviously Muslims from everywhere, bound on the pilgrimage... they were of all complexions, the whole atmosphere was of warmth and friendliness. The feeling hit me that there really wasn't any colour problem here. The effect was as though I had just stepped out of a prison" (*The Autobiography*, p433). His first steps on his spiritual journey were already shaking his core beliefs; all he had been taught in the NOI about the need for separation was being questioned.

Egyptian society was now eight years into the rule of General Gamal Abdul Nasser, who had seized power from the British with a base of support around Arab nationalism. Arab nationalism in this context was the identity of the oppressed. The idea of a common Arab identity was strengthened under colonial occupation in which Arabs were second class citizens. It cut through class divisions and united all Arab people in a common fight against their colonial rulers. The ideas later dovetailed with Ghanaian leader Kwame Nkrumah's pan-Africanism, a rallying call for the unity of all independent African nations under an anti-imperialist banner.

Pan-Africanism represented the hopes and desires that newly independent nations could form a powerful block against the West. It was centred on a belief that "African peoples, both on the continent and in the diaspora, share not merely a common history, but a common destiny" (exhibitions.nypl.org/africanaage/essay-pan-africanism.html).

At times the movement sounded radical and even revolutionary, but the demands of the working class were always superseded by the national interest. In the long term this suffocated the movements which had won independence in the first place. In the 1960s and 1970s, however, pan-Africanism was a beacon of freedom and represented the strength and resilience of the African people.

In Egypt Nasser implemented major reforms and won over large sections of Egyptian society. Malcolm notes the high level of industrialisation and public facilities which were built in order to position Egypt against the West in terms of development. This is something which would unfortunately be reversed under successive governments after Malcolm's death. The reforms which Nasser was able to put through were severely limited and running the state rather than uprooting it meant compromises were bound to be made.

Malcolm then travelled to Saudi Arabia in a plane packed with "white, black, brown, red and yellow people, blue eyes and blond hair, and my kinky red hair—all together, brothers" (*The Autobiography*, p436). During this experience and the intense spiritual awakening of Mecca, Malcolm converted to orthodox Sunni Islam. This was a formal denunciation of the Islam preached by the NOI. In Mecca Malcolm had to learn everything from scratch and was astounded by how little he knew.

As Malcolm travelled across Africa, under the influence of anti-colonial struggles, he began to form ideas around how to fight back against racism and drew the conclusion that capitalism was the problem; he famously said "you show me a capitalist; I'll show you a bloodsucker" (Speaking at the Audubon 1964, teachingamericanhistory. org/library/document/at-the-audubon/).

From this experience Malcolm was developing an idea of revolution and who has the power to change society. He saw revolutions as oppressed groups of people rose up en masse and took control of the state. His travels across Africa reinforced this as Black people, regardless of class, joined in mass demonstrations. He was using the language of socialism but what socialists agitate for is the self-emancipation of the working class and workers, Black and white, taking control of their lives.

Malcolm was kept separate from this vital element as he travelled across Africa. He was always in the company of national leaders or royalty and separated from ordinary people. His various speeches and addresses were to academics in universities or governments. This reinforced his standing as an international figure but took him away from grassroots struggles.

When he arrived in Ghana the country had been independent for seven years. In 1960 the Black Marxist writer C L R James announced: "today the centre of the world revolution is here in Accra" (Kent Worcester, *C L R James: A Political Biography*, State University of New York Press, 1996, p198). Kwame Nkrumah was the leader of the national struggle; he led a radical mass movement employing mass agitation, strikes, boycotts and riots.

Nkrumah was the leading theorist of pan-Africanism and is still immensely loved for his principled and uncompromising positions against capitalism and imperialism. After independence he declared: "the independence of Ghana is meaningless until it is linked with the total liberation of Africa" (panafricanquotes.wordpress.com/speeches/independence-speech-kwame-nkrumah-march-6-1957-accra-ghana/) and he set out to achieve a liberated United States of Africa in which all African nations had an equal say. He wanted independence from the economic control of European and US capital and believed the industrial strength of Africa could overshadow that of the West. However Nkrumah's emphasis on national unity blurred the argument of class division and by the time Malcolm arrived Ghana had become a one party state.

The state became the main vehicle for Pan African unity, but there was no defence for ordinary people when their interests came into conflict with it. During his stay in Ghana Malcolm was bussed from press appearances to key note speeches by a group of ex-pats including Maya Angelou who would later play a leading role in Black activism in the US. One of the stops in his busy schedule was a private meeting with Nkrumah where they discussed pan-African-ism. Malcolm argued the case of the African Americans and their place in the struggle. This planted the seed for the Organisation for Afro-American Unity (OAAU), as a parallel to the Organisation for African Unity (OAU), headed up by Nkrumah. Malcolm was forming a political basis for his new organisation by the time he reached Algeria.

In Algeria the Front de Libération National (FLN) had led a campaign of armed resistance to the French occupi-ers. The French state responded, especially after 1957, with intense repression: FLN leaders were hunted down and murdered. The focus of the FLN shifted to direct mili-tary confrontation and the fight became one that was controlled from the top down. But it was working class resistance and demonstrations in December 1960 that finally forced the French state to the negotiating table. When the French president, General Charles de Gaulle, visited for four days he sparked mass protests, riots and strikes; independence soon followed.

Algeria had one of the most profound effects on Malcolm. It showed him the struggle is not simply a racial conflict. He said: "I shall also tell them that what has been called the 'Negro Revolution' in the US is a deception prac-tised upon them, because they have only to examine the failure of this so-called revolution to produce any posi-tive results in the past year. I shall tell them what a real revolution means—the French Revolution, the American Revolution, Algeria to name a few. There can be no revo-lution without bloodshed" ("Message to the Grassroots").

In Algeria, however, as with many other African nations

there was certainty about who the oppressor was. In most cases an occupying European force was in military control. But in the US identifying the oppressors and those who had the power to fight them would be more difficult.

Swept up in a victorious atmosphere of African nationalism, Malcolm was propelled towards seeing socialism as the key to freeing Black people. He stated that "you can't have capitalism without racism" (George Breitman [ed], *Malcolm X Speaks: Selected Speeches and Statements*, Grove Weidenfeld, 1994, p91) and those who opposed racism and capitalism were usually socialists. However, the socialism which was promoted in the newly independent nations was a convenient way to describe their alliances with the Soviet Union in opposition to US imperialism. It also meant building up national industries through state ownership to be able to compete on a global scale. This guided Malcolm's idea of socialism and gave greater attention to the actions of the new governments rather than to the heroic struggles of the working class in the independence movements.

Malcolm was constantly looking for an alternative way forward to capitalism and its destruction of people's lives, and pan-Africanist socialism was providing the most progressive alternative. It was not only challenging colonialism, it was actually winning.

However, the new governments were tied into a system that forced them to compete on a global scale. As they were removed from the movement and attempted to represent the national interest the gains of the independence movements were lost and repressive measures against workers' rights were introduced. It is easy to look back on these struggles some 50 years later and offer a critique of the mistakes made. However, the courageous struggles of the African anti-colonialists were an inspiration to activists everywhere. It was not certain or evident at the time that they would fail to deliver real equality. The conclusions Malcolm would draw need to be seen in that context.

Later that year Malcolm returned to the US before setting out again for Africa. On this second trip he was hugely influence by the Mau Mau in Kenya. The Mau Mau fought a guerrilla war in the deep forests around Mount Kenya against British rule. An early leaflet described the militancy of the organisation: "We will fight them. Let those who have guns use them. Let those who have swords use them. And let those who have machetes, clubs and arrows use them." Their detachment from the rest of the population and the sheer number of British troops had defeated the Mau Mau by 1956. But the anger towards the British hadn't gone away. Unfortunately for the independence movement, Jomo Kenyatta took the reins. He betrayed the demands of the freedom fighters and built a close bond between his regime and the British.

By this point the FBI were following Malcolm wherever he went; they had been keeping a close eye on him since his police station stunt. They had extensive wire taps on his phones, reports from his trips to Africa and they had infiltrated the NOI. While Malcolm was in the NOI preaching separation he was watched from afar, but as his political development took him across post-colonial Africa it sent a shudder down the spine of the state. They latched onto him for fear he would follow in the footsteps of the revolutionaries and anti-imperialists in Africa.

★ 8: HOW TO ORGANISE

Malcolm announced the establishment of the OAAU and its charter at a public meeting in June 1964. He had enlisted the help of people who had been pulled into civil rights activity. Some were religious and drummed up support through churches in the South; others were pioneering new radicals from the SNCC. Recognising the diversity of the movement was a crucial step in building an organisation capable of exerting influence on the movement.

Malcolm had actually recognised the need for unity in order to push the civil rights movement forward during his time in the NOI. A few months before he was suspended he gave the speech "Message to the Grassroots" in which he said: "What you and I need to do is learn to forget our differences... You don't catch hell 'cause you're a Baptist, and you don't catch hell 'cause you're a Methodist... You catch hell 'cause you're a Black man... We have a common enemy... We have a common oppressor, a common exploiter, and a common discriminator. But once we all realise that we have this common enemy, then we unite on the basis of what we have in common. And what we have foremost in common is that enemy—the white man." By forming the OAAU he was applying that speech to the civil rights movement, but without the separatist language of the NOI.

A month after it was set up, a memo to FBI Director J Edgar Hoover described the OAAU as a threat to the national security of the US. The FBI had been watching Malcolm's development with caution and were now taking this organisation as a serious challenge.

Malcolm and John Henrik Clarke wrote the OAAU Basic Unity Program which covered four main sections: restoration, reorientation, education and economic security. Restoration was a targeted approach to restoring communication with Africa. Reorientation was turning towards understanding their African heritage and education would be the main tool employed by the OAAU to "liberate the minds of our children" and publish their own literature. Finally, economic security: "After the Emancipation Proclamation...it was realised that the Afro-American constituted the largest homogeneous ethnic group with a common origin and common group experience in the United States and, if allowed to exercise economic or political freedom, would in a short period of time own this country. We must establish a technician bank. We must do this so that the newly independent nations of Africa can turn to us who are their brothers for the technicians they will need now and in the future" (www.malcolm-x.org/docs/gen_oaau.htm).

The OAAU pushed for Black control of every aspect of their community and these echoes of Black Power were resonating louder as the civil rights movement moved forward. At the founding rally Malcolm stated that the organisation's principal concern was the human rights of Black people, but that it would also focus on voter

registration, school boycotts, rent strikes, housing reha-
bilitation, and social programmes for addicts, unwed
mothers, and troubled children. The Unity Program's aims
also talked about self-defence, something which would be
taken as a central point of the Black Power movement in
the coming years.

One of the main aims of the OAAU was to bring the
US in front of the United Nations and hold it to account,
with the help of other African nations. He didn't see
the US changing its ways without being pressured into
it by another force and because of the inspirational
anti-colonial struggles he saw those newly formed
independent nations being that force. However, the
colonisers were removed by people at the bottom of
society, not world leaders.

Malcolm was also being propelled forward by the
radical and sometimes revolutionary elements of the
civil rights movement, keeping him involved in the direct
actions and agitation against the government. So he was
being pulled by the two poles of resistance, the struggle
inside the system and the struggle outside.

The revolutionaries of the American Socialist Workers
Party (SWP)* saw Malcolm's transformation as a wel-
come step in the right direction and invited him regularly
to speak on platforms alongside trade unionists and
Marxists. This was at a time when most organisations
were keeping Malcolm at arm's length, knowing how
much the state was watching him and the baggage he
would bring from his past in the NOI.

Central to the American SWP was the effort to build

---

* The American SWP is not connected to the British SWP.

unity among the Black and white working class in order to smash capitalism. They believed bringing Malcolm closer to their organisation would not only win him to Marxist ideas but also win a new layer of Black activists who had been thrown into political activity around the civil rights movement.

During the final months of his life the American SWP became a strong defender of Malcolm's transformation and encouraged his political development.

★ 9: THE FINAL MONTHS AND VISITING BRITAIN

In Malcolm's final months the civil rights movement was in crisis and its momentum halted. Washington made it clear that no more reforms would be granted. The "freedom summer" of 1964, a voter registration drive in Mississippi, ended in mass arrests and murder. Meanwhile a series of urban uprisings began which would come to characterise the late 1960s and Black America.

In April 1964 Malcolm made his famous speech "The Ballot or the Bullet" which reflected the tensions within the movement. He argued for the right of all Black people to be able to vote, saying: "I'm not going to sit at your table and watch you eat, with nothing on my plate, and call myself a diner". He used the speech to describe the political power of Black people when voting, but also as a warning: "it's either the ballot or the bullet", meaning if change doesn't come after you've voted for it you can't sit around or wait for change. "Don't let anybody tell you anything about the odds are against you... they send you to Korea and make you face 800 million

Chinese. If you can be brave over there, you can be brave right here... And if you fight here, you will at least know what you're fighting for" ("The Ballot or the Bullet", 1964, Ohio. www.edchange.org/multicultural/speeches/malcolm_x_ballot.html).

At the end of 1964 and early 1965 Malcolm was speaking regularly alongside socialists, Black nationalists and integrationists trying to bring people together around a common goal of defeating racism. He was becoming an internationally renowned figure and increasingly travelling to speak abroad.

Malcolm visited the UK twice. The first time in December 1964 he debated at the Oxford Union and the second in February 1965 he went to Smethwick and gave a speech at Birmingham University. Britain in 1964 was witnessing one of the most racist elections in its history. Peter Griffiths, the Tory candidate in Smethwick, ran with the slogan: "If you want a nigger for a neighbour vote Labour" and the local Labour MP blamed immigration on the Tories and had their offices above a club which operated an informal colour bar, denying Black and Asian people entry.

Malcolm visited Oxford first to debate the topic "Extremism in defence of liberty is no vice; moderation in the pursuit of justice is no virtue". This highlighted arguments about self-defence and violence which the civil rights movement was trying to come to terms with. There is a common tendency to place Malcolm X and Martin Luther King Jr in opposition to each other, one violent and the other peaceful. But this is too simplistic a view. Neither was static. The tactics and determination of both King and Malcolm were necessary components of the movement and both changed depending on the circumstances of the time. Three years after the "I have a dream" speech King famously described the riots as "the language of the unheard" (www.crmvet.org/docs/otheram.htm). He also became an increasingly vocal opponent of the Vietnam War. Ideas change with material conditions and both Malcolm and King influenced and were influenced by the movement around them.

During his address to the Oxford Union Malcolm said: "anytime anyone is enslaved, or in any way deprived of his liberty, if that person is a human being, as far as I am concerned he is justified to resort to whatever methods necessary to bring about his liberty again." He used the speech to attack US imperialism by highlighting the assassination of Patrice Lumumba, Congolese independence leader and the first democratically elected leader of the Congo. This resonates strongly today with the hypocrisy of world leaders who use terrorism as an excuse for their own acts of terror. What Malcolm poses throughout the speech is the violence of the oppressed against the violence of the oppressor.

The second invitation to Britain came from Avtar Jouhl of the Indian Workers Association (IWA) and later a key figure in the anti-racist movement and in the Anti Nazi League (ANL).

When Malcolm came with the IWA to visit Smethwick he saw an entire other side of British life. There was a racist onslaught against Asian people and the frontlines of the fight were in Marshall Street, Birmingham. The Tory council supported a demand from white racists to buy any house that was put up for sale to stop non-whites moving in. This continued until eventually the Ministry of Housing banned it long after Malcolm's visit. Malcolm's agitational picture next to the Marshall Street road sign was a sign of international solidarity.

When Malcolm got back to the US, he was under huge pressure from the NOI and the FBI. He was regularly receiving death threats from the NOI; the FBI were well aware of this. Their extensive surveillance of Malcolm's life would have provided enough evidence to stop any possible attempts on his life, but the FBI did nothing. By the time Malcolm was killed the FBI had logged 41 files about Malcolm spanning more than 4,000 pages of text.

The day after Malcolm returned from the UK his house was burnt down.

His growing prominence as an uncompromising revolutionary with ties to independent African nations was an ever-greater thorn in the side of the state.

★ 10: ASSASSINATION AND LEGACY

Malcolm was cut down in his prime. In the 11 months between him leaving the NOI and his assassination he had already embraced ideas of internationalism and system change and rejected separatism. He showed that ideas can change, that no one is born a revolutionary and that the state can be shaken when we challenge it.

Malcolm was killed on 21 February 1965. He was shot several times at an OAAU rally at the Audubon Ballroom in Harlem, New York, leaving behind his wife, Betty, and six children—Qubilah, Ilyasah, Attallah, Gamilah Lumumba, Malikah and Malaak.

The men arrested for the crime were NOI members. There are many conspiracy theories surrounding his murder with many saying it was the FBI who pulled the trigger. Regardless of what is believed about Malcolm's killers, the state certainly allowed it to happen. On the night of the murder no one was searched for weapons, NOI members who had personally threatened Malcolm's life were there and there were armed FBI officers in the crowd and at the doors.

The state was scared of what Malcolm represented and they were happy to see him dead.

He correctly predicted that continued racism would

bring huge upheavals; riots erupted across the US only months after the March on Washington. The riots erupted around the major cities where tensions between Black people and the police were at their highest. Most significant were the Watts riots in south Los Angeles in August 1965.

Watts was a predominantly Black neighbourhood and the riots were sparked when tensions between the police and the local population reached breaking point.

A crowd of spectators gathered near the corner of Avalon Boulevard and 116th Street to watch two white police officers arrest a suspected drunk driver. The crowd were angry at what they believed to be yet another racist attack by the police. The heavy handedness of the police triggered riots by residents who were sick and tired of years of economic and political isolation. The local authorities only regained control with the help of the National Guard.

Over five days 34 people were killed, 1,032 injured, nearly 4,000 were arrested and US$40 million worth of property was destroyed. It was the most destructive urban riot in 20 years and foreshadowed rebellions in the ensuing years in Detroit, Newark and other US cities.

These riots were fuelled by the militancy and anger of a new emerging layer of activists who felt the pace of the civil rights movement was too slow. The Black Panthers and other Black nationalist groups were able to use this anger and direct it at the top.

The year of Malcolm's death and for the rest of the 1960s saw huge battles, and theories of challenging oppression were put to the ultimate test.

★ 11: THE BLACK PANTHERS AND DRUM

The radical spirit of Black Power, riots and rebellion that exploded in the late 1960s found expression through a number of organisations. The wider expression of growing anger against the Vietnam War was the backdrop for the rise of the Black Panther Party (BPP) and the Dodge Revolutionary Union Movement (DRUM). They were ignited by the struggle for civil rights and were able to radicalise layers of activists to challenge the system as a whole.

The BPP was set up at the end of 1966 by radicals who emerged from the civil rights movement led by Huey P Newton and Bobby Seale. Its core practice was to arm Black people to monitor the behaviour of police officers and challenge police brutality in Oakland, California. The BPP described themselves as revolutionaries and Marxists—which meant they orientated around the working class. However, they were heavily influenced by guerrilla resistance groups and when talking about the working class they focused on the "brothers on the block".

They were the most iconic and coolest organisation to emerge from the Black Power movement. Dressed all in black, with berets, guns and the Black Panther as an emblem, they were impossible to ignore.

They would "patrol the pigs" to protect Black people from police violence and of course the sight of Black men and women in uniform with guns struck fear into the heart of the police. This was an inspiration to people who had been beaten up and locked up during the riots. Arming yourself was seen as the viable alternative to fighting off the police with fists and for a short while they were safe in their own neighbourhoods. Unfortunately it also proved to be their undoing once the state went to war with the BPP. But in the short period of time it existed the BPP changed the lives of its members and followers, debating how to challenge other inequalities including gender, class and lesbian, gay, bisexual and transgender oppression as well as racism.

They had a ten-point programme which outlined an anti-capitalist approach to social and economic justice. The ten points were: for freedom, employment, an end to capitalist robbery, decent housing, an education of "our true history", against military service, for an end to police brutality and murder, "freedom for all Black men" in jail/prison and fair trials for Black people. The final point summed up a vision of a future society demanding land, bread, housing, education, clothing, justice and peace.

These demands appealed to ordinary people who were being victimised by a racist system. They are demands that are still being fought for today.

BPP support and membership grew through systematic campaigning in the northern ghettos and reaching out to the most disaffected Black people living in poverty. They set up a number of community and social programmes, but most famous was their free breakfast for children programme. It was a way of helping and providing for the local Black community where the state had failed them, but it was also a way of centring themselves in the community as respected activists.

Their programmes were hugely popular and won them respect across the US, but the state recognised them as a threat as soon as they were established. FBI Director J Edgar Hoover's reaction to the BPP mirrored his reaction to the OAAU: he called the party "the greatest threat to the internal security of the country".

At its height the BPP had approximately 10,000 members with many more supporters and a readership for their newspaper of 250,000. Their influence was enormous and a revolutionary movement of that size scared the state— so the state fought back ruthlessly. The FBI flooded crack cocaine into the ghettos and the law was amended to allow harsher sentences for crack cocaine than pure cocaine.

Key members of the BPP were assassinated and there were full-blown shoot-outs in the streets. They also played gangs off against the BPP and vice versa. Most significantly the FBI infiltrated and split the organisation from within. An atmosphere of paranoia was created that disabled sections of the BPP who ended up attacking each other rather than focusing their attention on the state.

Ultimately the revolutionary politics of the BPP were washed away as leaders and theorists left to take roles in local government or were murdered by the state. The BPP's focus on the most marginalised sections of the Black community and the substitution of a small committed band of professional revolutionaries for wider working class activity led them away from seeing the potential for self-emancipation in the working class, both Black and white.

While the BPP were focusing their activity in the Black community, DRUM was operating out of the car factories of Detroit with Black revolutionaries agitating within the working class. DRUM was formed in 1968 following a wildcat strike that showed workers' power in the workplace at the point of production. DRUM aimed to connect Black Power and workers' power. They led walk-outs, unofficial strikes and challenged the power of the bosses, winning demands and setting up other RUM groups in other car manufacturers including Ford and General Motors. During the period DRUM existed not a single member was shot at, put on trial or jailed—which really demonstrates the strength they held.

In 1969 the RUM groups came together to form the League of Revolutionary Black Workers. This was a significant step in forcing other trade unions to catch up and putting the bosses on the back foot. However, their reluctance to fight alongside white workers allowed the bosses to divide and rule, which weakened their movement and isolated them from huge numbers of sympathetic or revolutionary white activists.

Both the BPP and DRUM grew out of genuine anger and a desire to fight back, but a lack of clarity about where real power lay and the roots of racism proved fatal to both movements. The BPP's lack of engagement with the working class and DRUM's refusal to stand with white workers allowed the state to neutralise their potential. The question this poses, and which Malcolm X was fighting to answer, is how do we achieve real liberation?

★ 12: WHY DOES MALCOLM X REMAIN RELEVANT?

Malcolm's popularity is a tribute to the strength of the movement he represented. He is still someone we look up to when discussing militancy and is revered by almost everyone who looks to the civil rights struggle for inspiration.

Malcolm's speech at the Oxford Union opens a significant debate and exposes the reason why he was so hated by the state. He argued that the oppressed are justified in defending themselves and he understood that the system was rigged and would vilify the victims when they bit back.

Malcolm's reaction to a racist system is caricatured by those who compare him unfavourably to the peaceful Martin Luther King Jr. The truth is more complex. King was a courageous fighter, but he was prepared to work within the confines of the system. During the highest points of the movement the state saw King as a more manageable threat who at times could act as a restraint. It is because of this that we see the discussion about the two framed as if they were opposites. However, by the end of King's life he too spoke out more radically and was hunted by the state. Following the betrayals from Washington, King went so far to say: "Feeling that our demands were moderate, I had assumed that they would be granted with little question... This experience, however taught me a lesson. I came to see that no one gives up his privilege without strong resistance. I saw further that the underlying purpose of segregation was to oppress and exploit the segregated, not simply keep them apart" (Shawki, pp159-160).

Malcolm's ideas resonate today because unfortunately what he was saying in the 1950s and 1960s still rings true. After 50 years, despite great struggles, the situation of Black people is so bad that it has been considered necessary to march under the banner "Black Lives Matter". This is despite the fact that there are tens of thousands of Black people in positions of power, including in the White House itself. It is precisely because the gains of the civil rights movement have been driven back that people are searching for a new way forward.

By the time of his death Malcolm was actively searching for Black and white unity. It is important to recognise the great strides forward he made while also critically examining his mistakes so we aren't destined to repeat them. Both the BPP and Malcolm recognised that capitalism is the root of the racism they faced, but did not come to the conclusion that the working class is the agent of the change they wanted to bring about.

The legacy Malcolm left and that revolutionary socialists carry on today is to be tribunes of the oppressed, to fight against any injustice and to aim squarely at the top 1 percent who will always recycle oppression to suit their own interests.

We must fight like Malcolm "by any means necessary".

FURTHER READING

Saladin Ambar, *Malcolm X at Oxford Union: Radical Politics in a Global Era* (OUP USA, 2004)

Jack Barnes, *Malcolm X, Black Liberation and the Road to Workers Power* (Pathfinder Press, 2009)

George Breitman, *The Last Year of Malcolm X: The Evolution of a Revolutionary* (Pathfinder Books, 1970)

Alex Haley, *The Autobiography of Malcolm X* (Penguin, 2001)

Manning Marable, *Malcolm X: A Life of Reinvention* (Penguin, 2012)

Mark D Naison, *Communists in Harlem during the Depression* (University of Illinois Press, 2004)

Kevin Ovenden, *Malcolm X: Socialism and Black Nationalism* (Bookmarks, 1992)

Brian Richardson (ed), *Say it Loud: Marxism and the Fight Against Racism* (Bookmarks, 2013)

Ahmed Shawki, *Black Liberation and Socialism* (Haymarket, 2006)

Leon Trotsky, *Leon Trotsky on Black Nationalism and Self-Determination* (Pathfinder Press, 1994)

MORE BOOKMARKS REBEL'S GUIDES

A Rebel's Guide to James Connolly by Seán Mitchell (£3)
A Rebel's Guide to Eleanor Marx by Siobhan Brown (£3)
A Rebel's Guide to Rosa Luxemburg by Sally Campbell (£3)
A Rebel's Guide to Gramsci by Chris Bambery (£4)
A Rebel's Guide to Trotsky by Esme Choonara (£4)
A Rebel's Guide to Marx by Mike Gonzalez (£4)
A Rebel's Guide to Lenin by Ian Birchall (£3)
Sexism and the System: A Rebel's Guide to Women's Liberation by Judith Orr (£4)

Available from Bookmarks, 1 Bloomsbury Street, London WC1B 3QE
info@bookmarksbookshop.co.uk bookmarksbookshop.co.uk 020 7637 1848